FIRENZE
MVSEI

GREAT MASTERPIECES

MICHELANGELO

David

GIUNTI

Collection edited by: Gloria Fossi

Text by: Laura Ciuccetti

Translation by: Helen Cleary

Photographs: Rabatti-Domingie, Florence

By concession of the Ministero per i Beni Culturali e Ambientali of 13.2.1998. Reproduction by any means is strictly prohibited.

ISBN 88-09-21453-6

Michelangelo Buonarroti, *David*.
Marble, height 4.10m (the figure); 4.34m (including base).
Florence, Galleria dell'Accademia, Sculpture No. 1077.

Originally it was a block of marble, an enormous block of white marble, belonging to the Opera del Duomo of Florence, excavated with the intention of carving out a giant: a David or a Prophet for one of the buttresses of the Cathedral of Santa Maria del Fiore. Initially the work was entrusted to the sculptor Agostino di Duccio (1462) and later to Antonio Rossellino (1476) but both were forced to give up in face of the enormous technical difficulties. The block of marble was not compact, it was riddled with veins and above all it was tall and narrow, more suitable for slender gothic statues than for the muscular, active representations of Renaissance heroes. Leonardo da Vinci was also approached, and although he had a considerable experience in bronze sculpture, the artistic genius declined the offer and the roughly hewn block of marble was

forgotten in the courtyard of the Opera del Duomo until 1501. These were crucial years for the Florentine Republic. The Medici family had been expelled (1494) and the gonfalonier Pier Soderini was recalling the artists to give new impetus and backing to his government and to further the intellectual and artistic revival of the city. Michelangelo, informed by friends of the possibility of acquiring the great abandoned block of marble, also came back. For him, naturally obstinate, this opportunity of measuring himself against a generation of sculptors who had failed, together with the difficulties created by the previous "mutilations and damage", must have constituted a particularly intriguing challenge. Michelangelo was officially commissioned on 16 August 1501 at the age of 26. The enterprise took off immediately, and at the beginning of September the artist began testing the

solidity and quality of the block. In October he had a "turata di tavole" built around it, a kind of enclosure made of wood and masonry to protect and conceal his work. He must have made rapid progress since on 25 January 1504, after little more than two years, the enormous David was practically complete.

The work inspired considerable curiosity and admiration among the citizens, while to the artistic community which had known the original marble it seemed like "one raised from the dead". But the statue also kindled envy and criticism, and was from the very start the target of fanaticism and vandalism. In the biography devoted to Michelangelo, Giorgio Vasari relates how Pier Soderini, while on the whole full of praise for the statue, considered the nose too big. Pretending to heed him and to want to re-chisel the nose, the sculptor climbed onto the scaf-

folding judiciously scattering some marble dust which he had hidden in his fist. Only then did the gonfalonier grant his definitive approval, and, "as recompense", four hundred scudos. Given the exceptional nature of the work, a lively debate arose about its most suitable location: it was unthinkable to sacrifice this superb nude, moulded so as to be appreciated in the round, by flattening it against a wall, even if it were the wall of the imposing Duomo of Florence. A committee of the most famous artists of the time was therefore appointed. Giuliano da Sangallo and the now elderly Leonardo da Vinci suggested setting the statue up in the Loggia della Signoria, with the back wall darkened to enhance the whiteness of the marble. This solution, consistent with Leonardo's own studies of atmosphere and subtle shading was not, however, consistent with Michelangelo's ideas. His David was vi-

brant with a life of his own, and could certainly not be adapted for insertion in a "niche, blackened behind like some miserable chapel". Michelangelo was not present at the discussion but his desire, voiced by the herald of the Signoria, was to place his "giant" – as the Florentines called it – in front of the Palazzo della Signoria, the civic heart of the city, or at most in the courtyard of the Palazzo itself. The choice fell to the front of the Palazzo beside the great doorway: the severe rusticated facade would admirably set off the physical vitality of the David plastically defined in the white marble.

It was no easy matter to transport the heavy statue, which was more than four metres high, to Piazza Signoria, passing through the narrow and tortuous streets of Florence. Michelangelo and some of his ingenious friends designed and built **14** a special "castle" with winches and sturdy ropes

for the purpose. The journey took four days and to avoid acts of vandalism the statue was policed night and day by special guards; in spite of this it was the target of stone-throwing on the part of certain young louts (sadly, history repeats itself) who paid for their disrespect with a week of prison. On 8 June 1504 the "giant" reached the steps of the Palazzo della Signoria, but it was not raised onto its marble base and presented to the Florentines until 8 September, the feast of Our Lady. The crowd gathered in the square was impressed by the beauty of the colossal nude, but also by the iconographic originality. The Davids sculpted up until then had been generally inspired by the Biblical text, figures of young men clothed in tunics or drapery. A previous illustrious nude was Donatello's bronze (now in the Bargello Museum), but with a delicately adolescent body, adorned in the ancient manner with

sandals, sword and helmet. All the Davids had, however, been instructively represented with the macabre trophy of the severed head of Goliath at their feet. Michelangelo had instead conceived the image of a vigorous man, totally naked like an ancient hero or athlete with a glance which reveals a profound confidence in his own capacity. Because of his demonstrable physical and moral force, the David immediately came to embody in the imagination of the Florentines a symbol of civil virtue and a warning for the enemies of freedom. Subsequently even the academics have almost unanimously affirmed this civic quality in the David, while advancing different interpretations. Some have found links with the thought of Dante, others with the sermons of Savonarola, yet others with Neoplatonic thought. Most compelling is the

theory which sees the "giant" uniting within

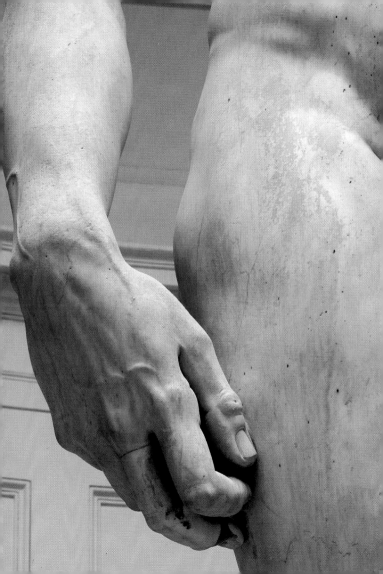

himself the qualities of David, the heroic biblical defender of the faith and of justice, and those of the figure of Hercules in classical mythology, symbol of strength sustained by intelligence.

After an act of vandalism which the statue suffered in 1527, Duke Cosimo I had it restored in 1543. Considering the civic significance of the statue, it might seem strange that the very monarch who had suppressed or undermined the power of the democratic institutions of the Republic contributed to its restoration. The duke's gesture, as well as expressing a sincere appreciation of Michelangelo, was an integral part of his political strategy. The figure of Hercules had been exalted since the times of Lorenzo il Magnifico, and Cosimo himself had more than once compared the acts of his government to the "Labours" of the mythical hero. He did not therefore attempt to distance the David from the

palace, which had in the meantime become his residence; on the contrary in ordering its restoration he put himself forward as the ideal restorer of civil peace. His ambiguity is revealed in his ordering of other colossi to place alongside it in the attempt to dilute its presence.

Exposed to the elements for centuries, by the mid nineteenth century the fragile and porous marble of the David was considerably deteriorated. In view of the fourth centenary of the artist's birth, it was decided to remove the work to the Accademia delle Belle Arti. In 1882 it was placed within a covered neo-Renaissance style tribune designed by the architect De Fabris, while a replica made by the copyist Arrighetti was put in its original position in Piazza Signoria. The removal to the Museum had the result of confirming its superiority in comparison to other statues, and, although abstracted from the

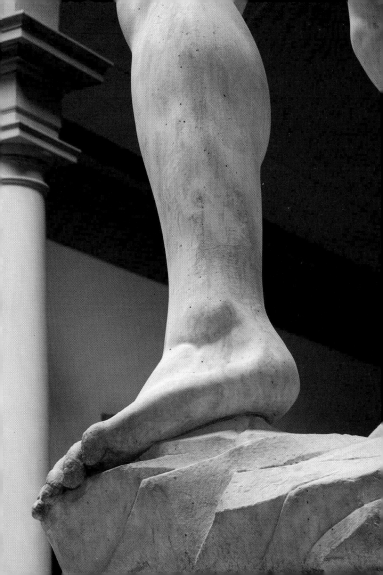

civic environment, it undoubtedly gained in terms of fame. An act of vandalism on the part of a maniac in September 1991, who attacked the toes of the left foot with a hammer, is an extreme example of the cult, or worse, of fanaticism which has grown up around the David. By now well-rooted in the collective imagination as an ideal of perfection, Michelangelo's David is the best-known sculpture in the world, a symbol of the art of all time. The first impression is that of a colossal naked body of an ancient athlete, or of a classically designed pagan god, perfect in anatomical form and proud of glance. But we must not stop at this first appearance; we must approach the work gradually, slowly circling it to discover from a multitude of angles, the many men, heroes and myths which it contains. The sculpture we have in front of us does not show a youth in a static, relaxed and triumphant pose,

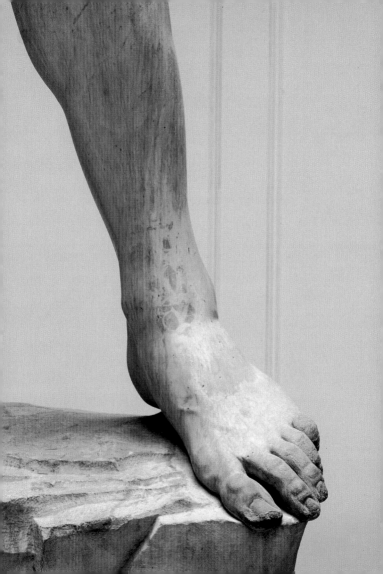

nor a warrior caught in the strain of battle, as he was wont to be described with anatomical virtuosity in the second half of the fifteenth century. David, the young Jewish shepherd is for Michelangelo an already mature man, and the artist depicts him in the moment before the launching of the stone with which he is to strike the Philistine giant, at a climax of mental concentration and physical tension. If, without embarrassment, we try to imitate his posture, and with legs slightly apart put our weight on the right, the left knee flexes forwards almost automatically, creating an attitude of "reflection" which raises the left shoulder and the right buttock. Up to this point the body remains balanced. Now let's pretend that we are grasping the sling (a catapult with a leather band) which is resting on our shoulder, in our left hand, and gripping a stone in our right, the wrist tensely

clenched like that of the statue, and move the left foot forward (as can be clearly observed from the back view of the statue). This position cannot be held for more than a moment... there follows immediately a transfer of weight to the ball of the left foot, the twisting of the trunk and the launch of the stone in the direction upon which the figure's glance is focused. The head set upon the strained neck is turned, as if abruptly, towards the left (in medieval illustration danger always approached from this side). It's not easy to speak of the beauty of David's face. To appreciate his expression we have to circle him slowly, discovering at each step and from each angle what he reveals: not a single face, but rather a series of faces, of increasing intensity. Standing in front of the statue we see only the classic profile conveying a sense of thoughtful composure. But

when we move around it we observe how this

expression is intensified, contracted to the point of menace in the glance directed at the enemy. What we have before us is not therefore a detached and heroic attitude, but one which is much more human and intimate. The very defects contribute to this earthly dimension: as one gets closer, in fact, David's head and hands begin to appear out of proportion. This is an effect deliberately designed to accentuate those parts of the body connected with Thought and Action. Had it been executed according to the classical canons the face would never have shown the same intensity, and the power of the hands would have vanished. Although Michelangelo had a profound knowledge of anatomy, based on his studies of antiquity and real life observation, he goes beyond theoretical rules, elaborating and disregarding them to highlight moral expression.

Michelangelo and the story of the David

1475 He is born in Caprese (Arezzo) on 6 March.

1488-92 After his apprenticeship in Ghirlandaio's workshop, he frequents the Medici circle, and studies classical sculpture. First works in marble: the *Battle of Centaurs and Lapiths* and the *Madonna of the Steps* (Casa Buonarroti Museum).

1494-98 Sojourns in Venice, Bologna and Rome. He sculpts the *Bacchus* of the Bargello and enters into a contract for the Vatican *Pietà*.

1501 Entrusted with the execution of the David by the Florentine Republic.

1507 Paints for Angelo Doni the *Holy Family* now in the Uffizi (Tondo Doni).

1508-12 Frescoes the ceiling of the *Sistine Chapel*.

1513 Sculpts the *Dying Slave* and the *Rebel Slave* (Louvre) and the *Moses* for the funeral monument of Julius II in Rome.

1519 Commissioned by Leo X for the New Sacristy in the church of San Lorenzo in Florence. Begins the *Prisoners* (Galleria dell'Accademia).

1524-26 Begins work on the Laurentian Library and on the sculptures for the Medici Chapels (*Twilight, Dawn, Night and Day*).

1527 The *David* is damaged during a popular revolt against the Medici. Fragments of the left arm and hand remain on the ground for three days. The artists Giorgio Vasari and Francesco Salviati gather them up and preserve them until 1543.

1543 Cosimo I has the left arm and hand of the *David* restored.

1553 Begins work on the Pietà for the Duomo of Florence.

1564 Michelangelo dies in his house in Rome on 18 February.

Bibliography

A. Condivi, *Vita di Michelangelo. Buonarroti (1553),* edited by E. Spina Barelli, Milan 1964.

G. Vasari, *La Vita di Michelangelo nelle redazioni del 1550 e 1568,* edited by P. Barocchi, 4 volumes, Milan-Naples 1962.

G. Vasari, *Le Vite dei più eccellenti pittori, scultori, architetti...,* edited by R. Bettarini and P. Barocchi, Florence 1987.

Ch. De Tolnay, *Michelangelo,* Princeton 1945-1960.

G.C. Argan, B. Contardi, *Michelangelo,* dossier, «Art e Dossier», no. 9, Florence 1987.

G. Cosmo, *Michelangelo, la scultura,* dossier, «Art e Dossier», no. 125, Florence 1997.

AA.VV., *Michelangelo, L'Ottocento, L'Accademia,* edited by F. Falletti, Livorno 1997.

Printed in June 1998 by Giunti Industrie Grafiche S.p.A., Prato